ON THE HUNT

TURKEY HUNTING

BY ROXANNE TROUP

EPIC

BELLWETHER MEDIA • MINNEAPOLIS, MN

EPIC BOOKS are no ordinary books. They burst with intense action, high-speed heroics, and shadows of the unknown. Are you ready for an Epic adventure?

This edition first published in 2025 by Bellwether Media, Inc.

No part of this publication may be reproduced in whole or in part without written permission of the publisher. For information regarding permission, write to Bellwether Media, Inc., Attention: Permissions Department, 6012 Blue Circle Drive, Minnetonka, MN 55343.

Library of Congress Cataloging-in-Publication Data

LC record for Turkey Hunting available at: https://lccn.loc.gov/2024037678

Editor: Elizabeth Neuenfeldt Designer: Jeffrey Kollock

Printed in the United States of America, North Mankato, MN.

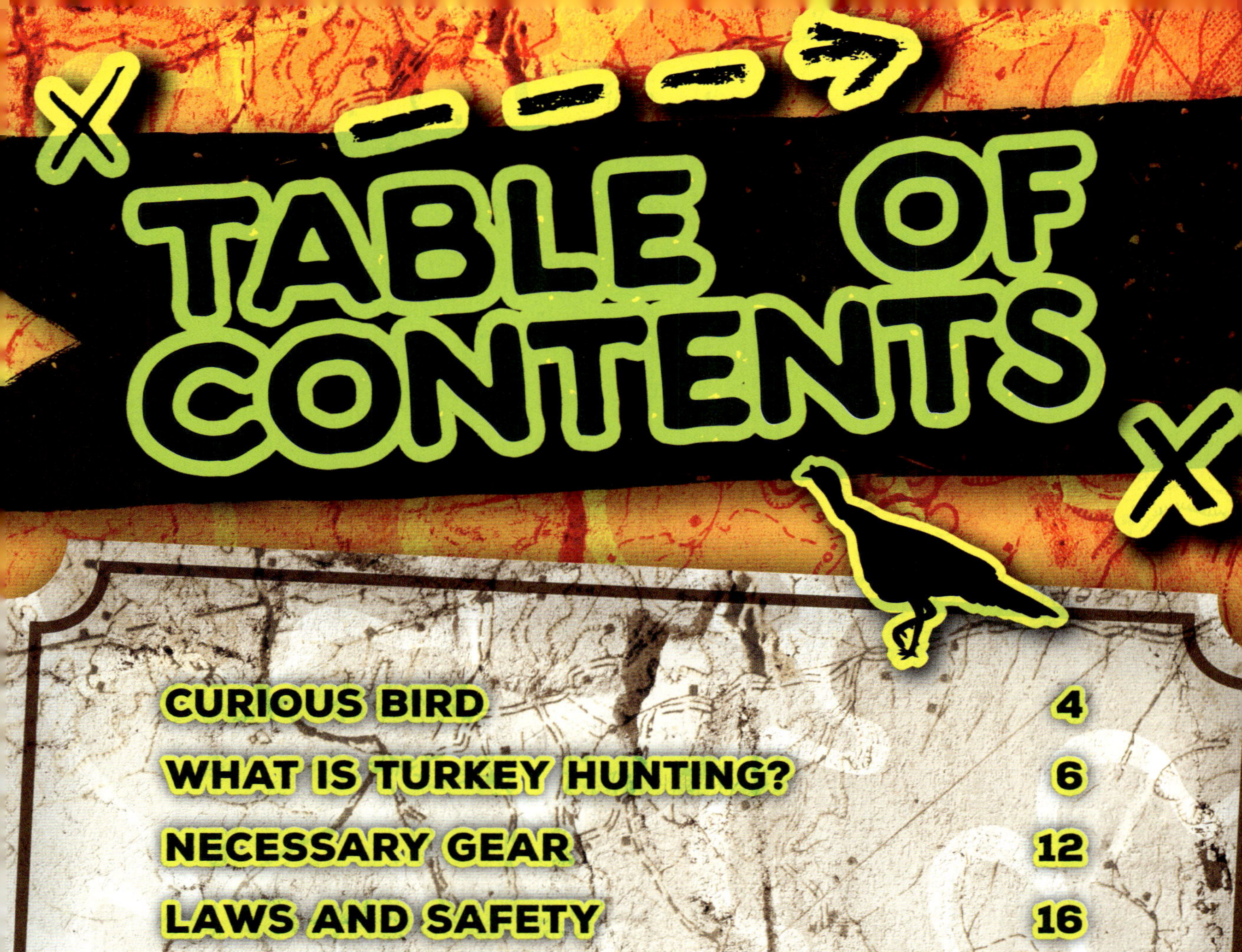

TABLE OF CONTENTS

CURIOUS BIRD

A hunter waits in the brush. A **tom** calls nearby. The hunter responds. The hunter's call sounds like a **hen**.

The tom peeks over a log. The hunter calls again. The tom comes close. Boom! A clean shot!

WHAT IS TURKEY HUNTING?

Turkeys live in forests throughout North America. They **roost** in trees but eat in fields.

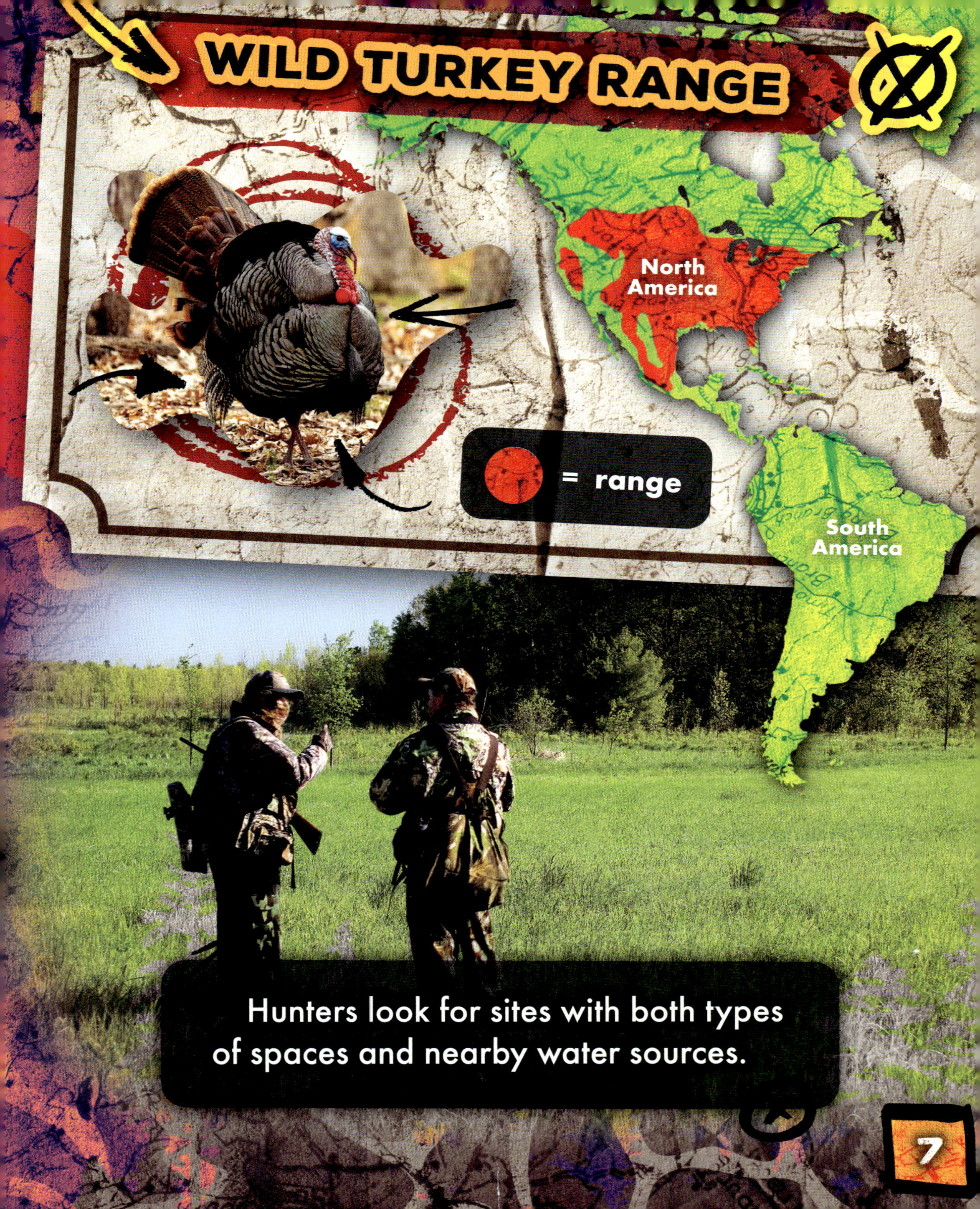
WILD TURKEY RANGE
North America
South America
= range
Hunters look for sites with both types of spaces and nearby water sources.

People hunt turkeys in the spring and fall. In spring, only **bearded** turkeys can be **harvested**. Hens are nesting.

SCAT FACT
Male and female turkeys poop different shapes! Male turkey poop is shaped like a J. Female poop is a spiral.
harvesting
In fall, both toms and hens can be harvested.

Many people hunt turkeys for food. Turkey feathers are used for decorations.

Hunters also enjoy the outdoors. They work hard to master the **turkey call**. When a turkey responds, it is exciting!

FAVORITE HUNTING SPOT

SHANNON COUNTY, MISSOURI

- Over **156** square miles (404 square kilometers) of public hunting land
- Over-the-counter hunting permits

turkey call

NECESSARY GEAR

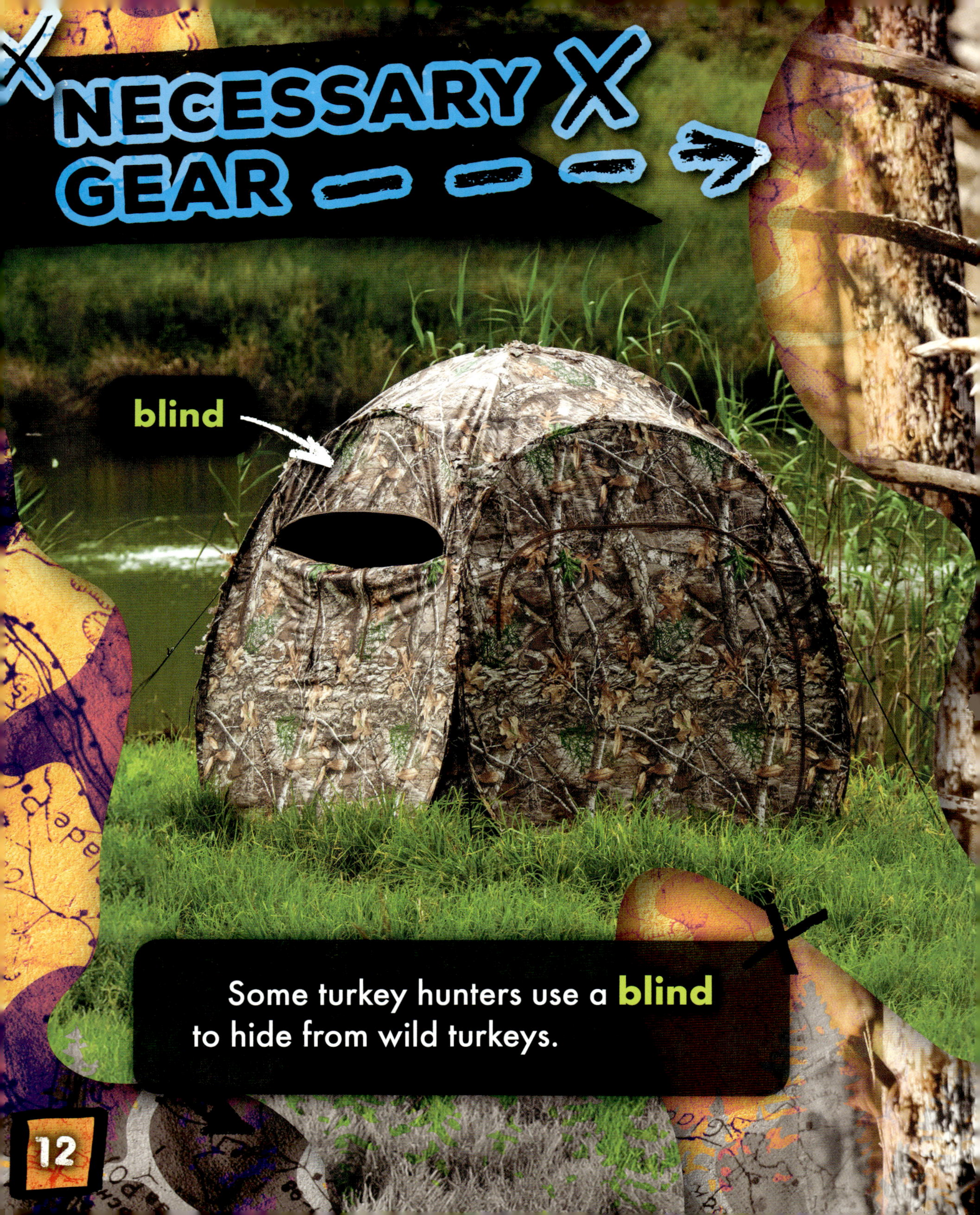

Some turkey hunters use a **blind** to hide from wild turkeys.

Others depend on **camouflage**.
They also hide their faces behind brush.

Turkey hunters use **decoys** and turkey calls to draw in birds. Most use a shotgun to get their turkey. Others use a bow.

Turkey vests can be helpful. Hunters carry calls, **nontoxic ammo**, and other supplies in their pockets.

LAWS AND SAFETY

Turkey hunters need to buy a **license** to hunt. Licenses limit the number of turkeys a hunter can harvest.

License fees help states **conserve** wild lands.

Several hunters may share the same hunting space. Safety is important.

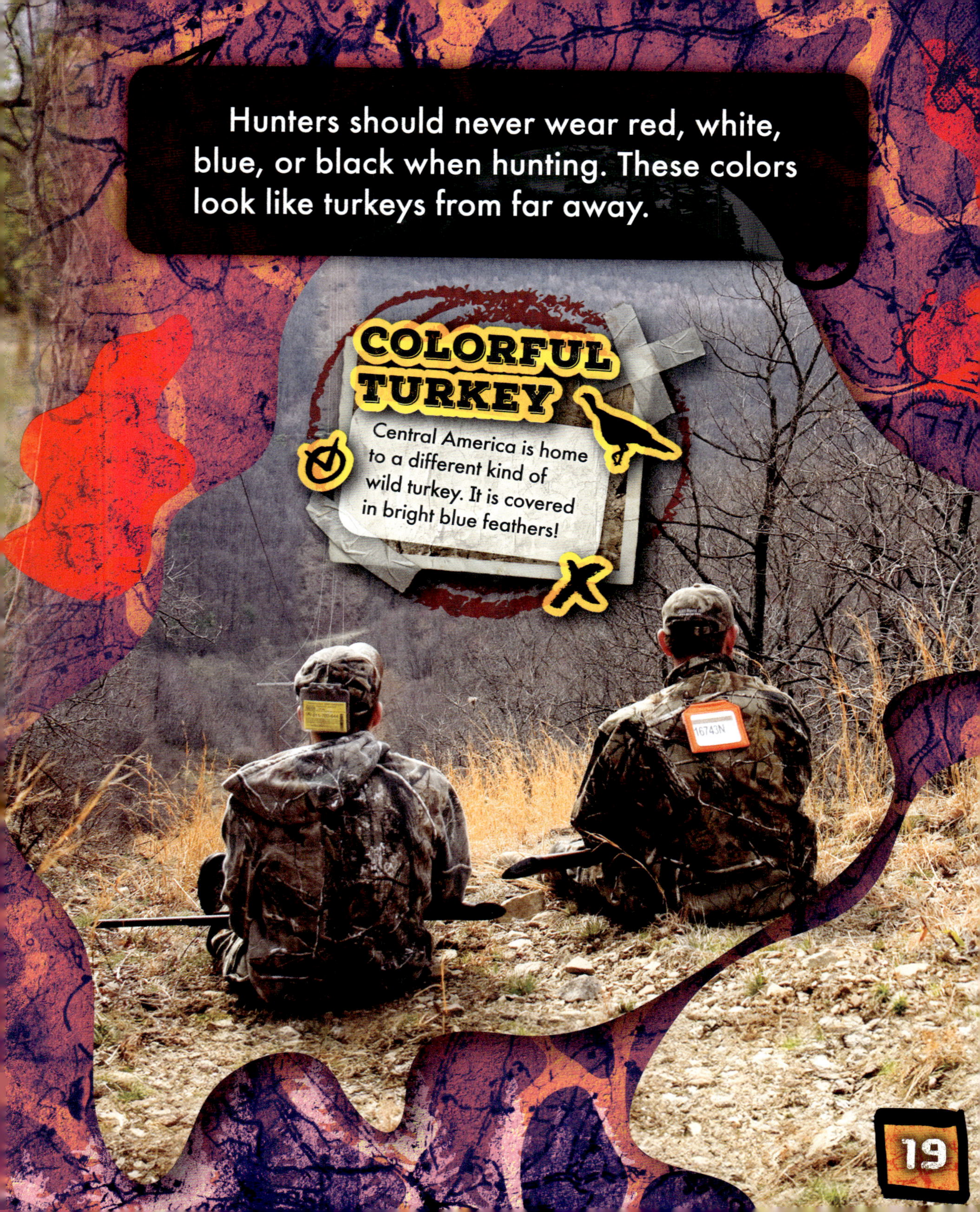

Hunters should never wear red, white, blue, or black when hunting. These colors look like turkeys from far away.

COLORFUL TURKEY

Central America is home to a different kind of wild turkey. It is covered in bright blue feathers!

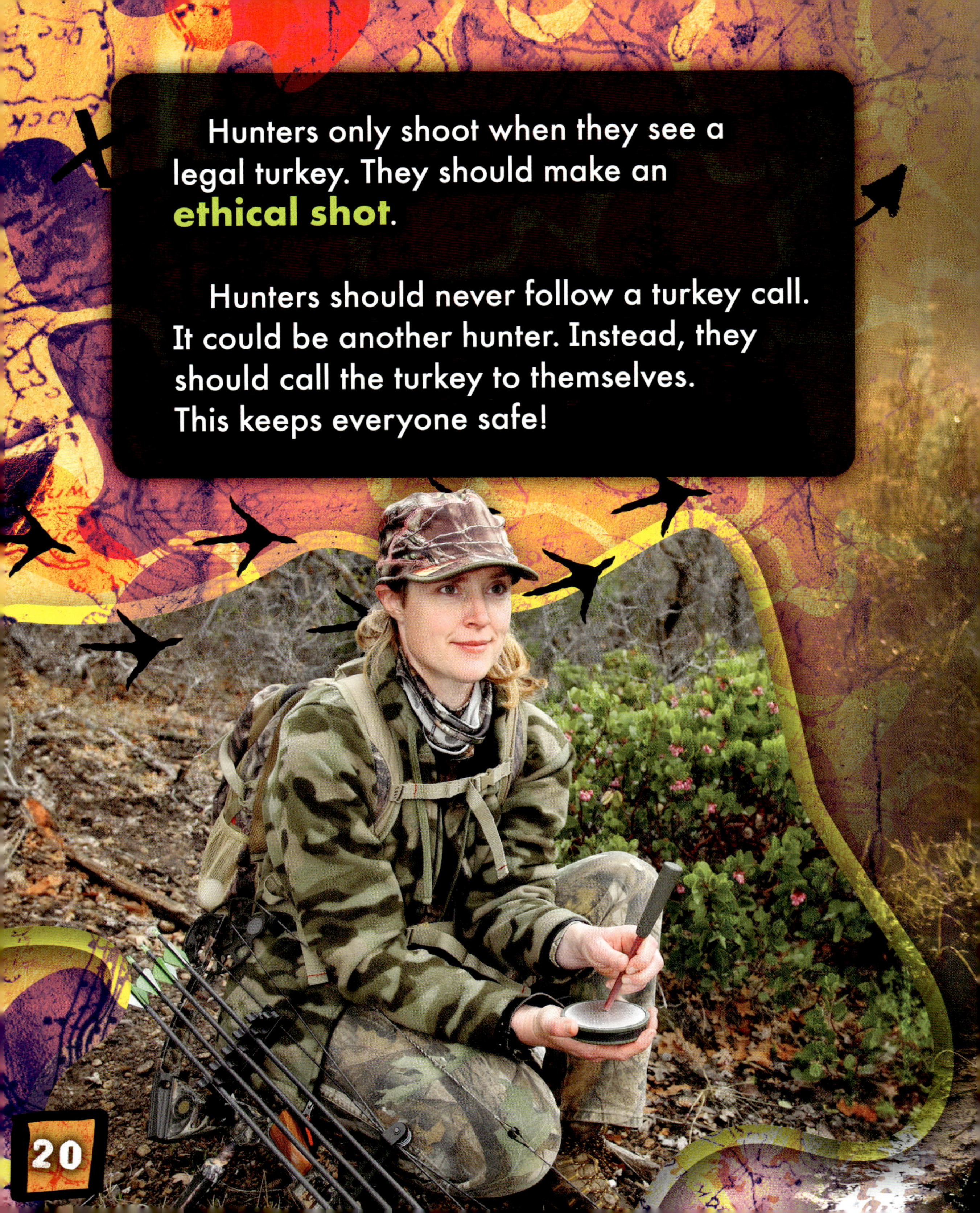

Hunters only shoot when they see a legal turkey. They should make an **ethical shot**.

Hunters should never follow a turkey call. It could be another hunter. Instead, they should call the turkey to themselves. This keeps everyone safe!

GLOSSARY

bearded—a turkey with hair-like feathers that hang from the chest; typically, only male turkeys have a beard.

blind—a small hut or closed space in which hunters wait

camouflage—a fabric that uses colors and patterns to blend in with surroundings

conserve—to take care of the environment

decoys—models of turkeys used to attract real turkeys

ethical shot—a clean shot that reduces pain and suffering to an animal

harvested—collected

hen—a female turkey

license—a document that gives hunters legal permission to harvest a certain type of animal

nontoxic ammo—ammo made with material that is not poisonous to animals

roost—to rest or sleep

tom—a male turkey; a tom is also called a gobbler.

turkey call—a noisemaker that copies the sounds female turkeys make

TO LEARN MORE

AT THE LIBRARY

Bailey, Diane. *Bird Hunting*. Minneapolis, Minn.: Lerner Publications, 2024.

Roe, Monica. *Turkey Hunt Tradition*. North Mankato, Minn.: Capstone, 2021.

Troup, Roxanne. *Duck Hunting*. Minneapolis, Minn.: Bellwether Media, 2025.

ON THE WEB

FACTSURFER

Factsurfer.com gives you a safe, fun way to find more information.

1. Go to www.factsurfer.com.
2. Enter "turkey hunting" into the search box and click 🔍.
3. Select your book cover to see a list of related content.

INDEX

The images in this book are reproduced through the courtesy of: ranchrunner, cover; photomaster, p. 3; Gregory Crosby Jr, p. 4; Danita Delimont, p. 4 (hen); thangs1, p. 5; Jeffrey B. Banke, pp. 6, 15, 23; James Smedley/ Alamy, p. 7; Nahian Aronno, p. 7 (range); Bruce MacQueen, p. 8; Steve Oehlenschlager/ Alamy, p. 9; Jeffrey S. Adams/ Alamy, p. 11; Tosh Brown/ Alamy, p. 11 (turkey call); Robert Wedderburn, p. 12; Design Pics Inc/ Alamy, p. 13; Nikita Rogul, p. 13 (camouflage); Kerry Hargrove, p. 14; BearFotos, p. 15 (shotgun); David DeFillipo, p. 15 (decoy); Stefan Malloch, p. 15 (camouflage); enterlinedesign, p. 15 (turkey call); Cavan Images/ Alamy, p. 16; John Edward Callahan, p. 17; ZUMA Press Inc/ Alamy, p. 18; David Troy/ Alamy, p. 19; Nathan Allred/ Alamy, p. 20; Roman Kosolapov, p. 21.